North American Indian Silver Craft

North American
INDIAN
Silver Craft

E. Pauline Johnson
(Tekahionwake)

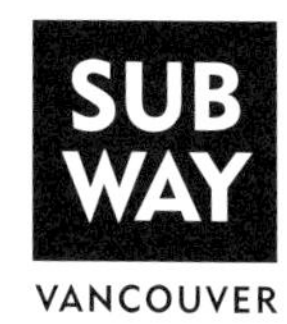

with Westcoast Words

National Library of Canada Cataloguing in Publication

Johnson, E. Pauline (Emily Pauline), 1861-1913
North American Indian silver craft / E. Pauline Johnson (Tekahionwake).

ISBN 0-9687163-7-7

1. Indian silverwork—North America. 2. Indians of North America—
Jewellery. I. Title.
E98.S55J63 2004 739.27'089'97
C2004-900298-8

Subway Books Ltd.
1819 Pendrell Street, Unit 203
Vancouver, B.C. V6G 1T3, Canada
E-mail: *subway@interlog.com*
Website: *www.subwaybooks.com*

in association with:
Westcoast Words
3036 Waterloo Street
Vancouver, B.C. V6R 3J6, Canada
Website: *www.westcoastwords.com*

Editing: Pamela Robertson
Design and production: Jen Hamilton
Cover Photo: M410, Gorget; Aboriginal; Iroquois, about 1817-1828.
McCord Museum of Canadian History, Montreal, used by permission.

Canadian orders:
Customer Order Department
University of Toronto Press
5201 Dufferin Street
Toronto, Ontario M3H 5T8, Canada
E-mail: *utpbooks@utpress.utoronto.ca*
Toll-free Tel.: 1-800-565-9523
Toll-free Fax: 1-800-221-9985

US orders:
University of Toronto Press
2250 Military Road
Tonawanda, New York 14150
Tel.: (716) 693-2768
Fax: (716) 692-7479

FOREWORD

E. Pauline Johnson, also known as Tekahionwake, was a poet, short story writer, essayist—and celebrity. In the last years of the 19th century and the first of the 20th, she was the most famous living writer of Indian ancestry, known to readers in the United States, Britain and especially her native Canada, through her books and public readings.

She was born in 1861 on the Six Nations Reserve at Brantford, southwest of Toronto, and her ancestry was impressive. Her father, a Mohawk elder statesman, was descended from Molly and Joseph Brant, siblings who were two of the most important Iroquois leaders of the late 18th century. The family of her mother, who was white, was equally distinguished and included the novelist William Dean Howells.

Some regarded Johnson as an authority on Native culture but at times she felt as much an outsider among Natives as among whites, who referred to her admiringly as the "Indian poetess." Indeed, she spent her entire life walking a tightrope between the white and the Native worlds. Her predicament seemed to be symbolized by the fact that, on her long and hugely successful personal appearance tours, she wore a version of Native attire during the first part of the show but changed into a middle-class mainstream outfit for the second. Her audiences were usually white, and they found her a person of enormous charm and charisma.

In 1908, with her writing and performing career in decline, Johnson moved to Vancouver, where she long had had a loyal following. She supported herself by journalism, including a series of articles on "The Silver Craft of the Mohawks" published in an obscure American magazine, *The Boys' World*, between April and December 1910. They were illustrated with her own drawings, which are reproduced here.

When, that same year, Johnson was diagnosed with breast cancer, her Vancouver friends attempted to raise money for her by collecting and publishing more of her work in book form. The best known of these volumes is *Legends of Vancouver*, whose retelling of traditional stories closely resembles the approach in the following pages. Johnson's pieces on Mohawk silver may have been intended as another such eleventh-hour project, for she slightly reworked and reorganized the material. The present edition is based on her revised manuscript, which found its way to the Vancouver Museum after her death in 1913 (which occasioned the largest funeral the city had ever witnessed).

Johnson's manuscript bears no title. The one we have supplied takes into consideration the fact that the writer not only has been undergoing a revival in Canada but also that interest in her is growing in the United States as well. Hence the phrase "Native American" rather than "First Nation," the preferred term in Canada. In the text itself, we have adhered to Johnson's (and the magazine's) style and usage, which were those of the time. Certainly no one would use such phrases as "red Indian races" today.

Little else has been written on the silver craft of Native people in the northern part of North America. This fact, as much as the ongoing reappraisal of Pauline Johnson and her contribution to the understanding of Native ways, seems to us more than sufficient reason for making these writings available in permanent form nearly a century after they first appeared.

THE PROTECTIVE TOTEM

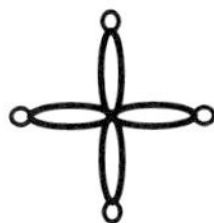

THE RED INDIAN RACES have always been workers in metals, and the earliest records show that in their most primitive savagery, they compelled the earth, as well as the forest, to yield them material whereby they might gain a living. Flint arrowheads were the main weapons of bringing down big game for food, but these were frequently supplanted by arrowheads of beaten copper. Sliver was seldom used except for ornamentation, but so deep a meaning was always attached to the "white metal," as many tribes called it, that it finally became of the greatest importance, and ornaments made of it and worn by chiefs and warriors marked their standing and position in the tribe as decidedly as the eagle plume of power, or the string of scalps of conquest.

Since the white man came with his silver coin the Indians have almost ceased to work the virgin metal into totems or ornaments. For two hundred years they have hammered, bent, beaten, and melted the already refined coin to suit their own uses. Certain men among the Mohawks have made a life trade of silver craft. The father works at it until he is an old, old man, his son follows in the same business, and his grandson begins to learn the trade while he is yet a very little boy. One family has worked at it for so many generations that their surname is now legally

"Silversmith." There is "Old John" Silversmith, "Young John" Silversmith and little "Alick" Silversmith—three generations bearing a name that has been earned honestly and creditably because of splendid workmanship and fine industry.

Among the Mohawks "brooches" are the particular ornaments to be manufactured by the slim agile fingers of the silversmiths. Bracelets, head-bands and earrings are worn by men as well as women. But the silver brooch with its unusual fastening is the one thing that must never be omitted from your costume if you make any pretense at all to distinction among your fellow-men. The designs of these brooches are so ancient that they are now of great historical value, and a matter of not only family pride but tribal tradition.

The foremost national design of the Mohawk brooches is without question the heart. In almost every one of the scores of curious and beautiful patterns the heart can be traced. If carefully examined, every brooch reveals some suggestion of this heart. Added to this a large percentage of the brooches display the form of an owl, or something that suggests the bird—its eyes, its claws, its "horns," the shape of its body—and one of the first lessons an Indian boy who desires to learn silver craft is, to design his own patterns, which, however fantastic he may make them, *must* reveal a heart or an owl cunningly "woven" through the bolder pattern. If he can succeed in combining the two, he is regarded as indeed an expert. The Mohawks hold that the heart means the strength of life of all races and nations, but the owl belongs to their own particular people. It is the guardian of their council fires; it watches over the smoldering embers through the night hours, for its extraordinary eyes see better in the dark than in the daylight; and it wards off evil and strife and meanness from approaching the great affairs of the nation. It protects the lawmakers from thinking of themselves instead of the people, it guards the counselors from doing things for their own personal benefit instead of for the lasting good of the nation. Its keen sight can discover evil coming out of the dark, and it stands between that evil and the chiefs and braves and warriors, so that the council fire may always burn in a clear, clean, sinless, pure flame.

It is called the "Protective Totem," or the "Guardian Owl."

Our illustration gives one of the most ancient designs of silver brooches. It is called the "Wolf of the Council Fire," the Wolf "Clan" and Totem being the most aristocratic in the Mohawk tribe. In dissecting this brooch one can unearth many a "buried treasure." The space in the center represents the Council Fire, the bars immediately enclosing it stand

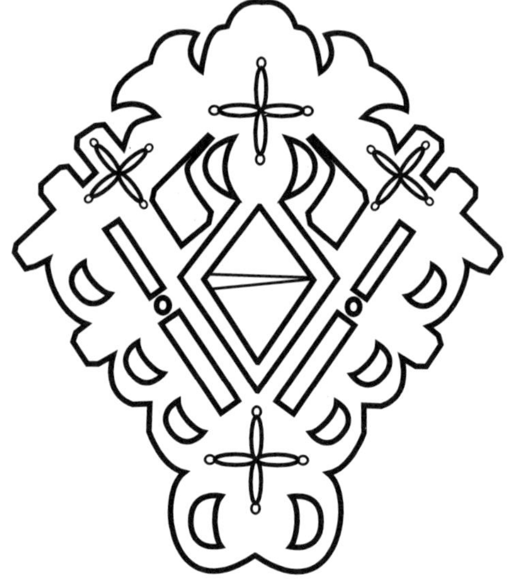

THE PROTECTIVE TOTEM

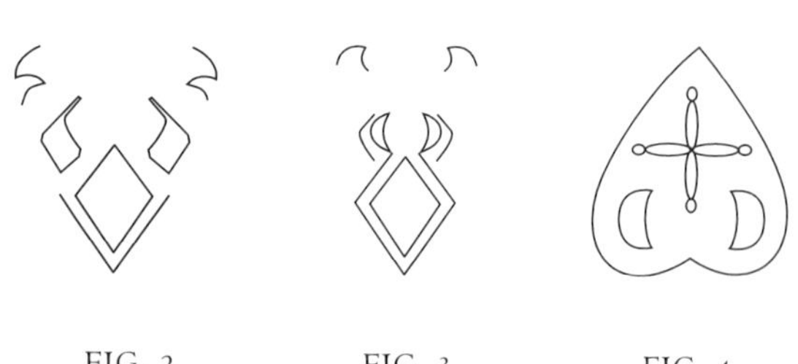

FIG. 2 FIG. 3 FIG. 4

for the fire-keepers, the outside bars are the chiefs, and the edges of semicircles, or scallops, indicate the braves and warriors arrayed in war paint ready to do and die in defense of their ancient government. In Illustration No. 2 a suggestion of the wolf's head can be seen. No. 3 shows the horned owl; the center of the owl's breast, where its heart is supposed to be, is also the exact position of the Council Fire. The owl's ever watchful eyes peer out immediately above it. The whole is based on an inverted heart (No.4). If the reader will cut out these drawings he will find they fit exactly one over the other, yet with all its apparent simplicity the brooch is teeming with design and meaning. The identical brooch from which the writer made these sketches was beaten from coin many years before the American Revolution, when the Mohawks lived in the Mohawk Valley in New York State. In that war they sided with the Mother Country, and fought for King George against the Colonists. During these stormy years the Mohawks, following the custom of their ancestors, buried their treasure for safe-keeping. Pounds and pounds of these solid silver brooches were hidden in the earth near Niagara Falls, and when the United States declared their independence, these red-skinned loyalists exhumed their valuables and brought them into Canada, which was still the king's domain, and where immense grants of lands were given them as reward for adhering to "The Crown." This brooch was one of the "buried" many, which the Mohawks treasure today as other natives treasure jewels. Perhaps the most beautiful thing about this particular brooch is the fact that a boy need not wait to grow up into a warrior before he can have the right to make or wear it. He has not got to be the son of a chief, or to win his eagle plume, or to be known as a mighty hunter, before he pins this significant emblem on his buckskin shirt or his soft turban. He may be young, poor, unsuccessful, untitled, but with Mohawk blood in his veins he has as much right to wear this great national badge as has the most powerful chief of his tribe.

THE BROOCH OF BROTHERHOOD

THE MOST GRACEFUL DESIGN that Mohawk fingers have ever fashioned from silver is the double heart surmounted by a crown. A single heart, when curved or crooked, has a dark and deplorable meaning. It is known as "The Traitor's Token," which we shall discuss in a later chapter, but when *two* hearts are entwined, they may be curved at will, and yet bespeak the best and most beautiful things in the lives of men.

Perhaps two tribes have been at war, or two clans have stirred up half forgotten feuds. The Wolf Clan may be warring on the Bears, or the Bears on the Turtles, but when the dawn of peace breaks once more through the shadows of the wilderness, the mighty warriors light their peace-pipes and request the silversmiths to beat from the white metal this brooch of brotherhood, and the scalping knife is loosened from the belt, the tomahawk is buried, and this beautiful badge of concord is worn in their stead.

It does not require a very imaginative eye to see that the center of the brooch formed by the curve of the two hearts is the breast of our old friend the owl, that the small center perforation in the crown is his beak, and that his two wonderful eyes gleam above it. In fact, there are three owl heads craftily grouped in this crown. If you take a pencil and with a deep mark close the gaps in the

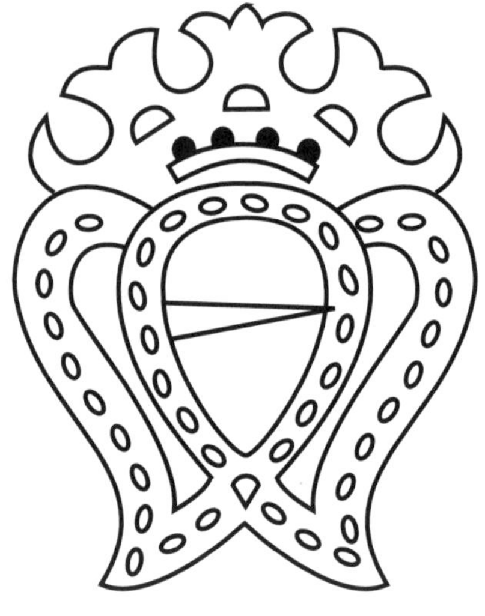

THE BROOCH OF BROTHERHOOD

crown, you will more easily detect the owls' faces. The center owl's eyes do duty, forming the right and left eyes of the side owls, but each has his own beak. The bodies of the side owls are formed by the two whole hearts, and when your eye grasps the outline you will find they look as if their heads were tilted on to their shoulders.

Here again we find the "Protective Totem" guarding the entwined hearts of peace, hearts that have been bent and distorted by strife and warfare, but now mingle as one under the crown of brotherhood. A curious story is connected with this brooch. Many ages ago, before the white man ever sailed up what is now the Hudson River, a very brave young hunter followed the trails of the forest from lake to river, and from river to sea. He could overcome the fiercest bull moose, capture the wary lynx, the treacherous wildcat, he could wrestle with the strongest bear, outwit the keenest fox, and slay the stealthiest wolf. He was very young, very strong and very noble. It was he who supplied all the old and sick of his tribe with the meat of the forest, with soft furs for their beds and silky pelts for garments. The people loved him, for his heart was as true as his aim, his words as straight as his arrow. He had but one enemy on earth, a sullen, ferocious chief, twice his own age, but whose eagle plume hardly reached the tip of the young hunter's ear. This chief was continuously on the warpath. His two greatest pleasures seemed to be bloodshed and jeering and gibing at the hunter because of his peaceful occupation.

"Keeper of old men, feeder of old women," he would sneer as the hunter would take his bow and arrows and start forth in search of food for the foodless. But the boy would only laugh, and reply, "Watch yourself, oh mighty warrior. I am many fingers taller than you. Watch lest some day I fight not the Delawares as you do, but fight you of my own tribe."

Then his enemy would scoff tauntingly, "*You?* You can only fight bears and foxes, not *men*."

Then when the hunter would only laugh and take the forest trail, his friends would take up his cause, and in their turn would sneer at his enemy, and say, "Yes, you can fight men, but does that feed the grandsires of the tribe who are as children, unable to roam the forest for food? Even you, mighty as you are, have not the quick eye, the cunning brain, to entrap wild animals to feed yourself. You would starve in the wilderness did you not go killing Delawares and plundering their lodges for food. *You* could not battle a bull moose and bring home its meat—for food you must kill a foe, and eat the meat his women cook, or else come home and eat our venison, that other men wise in the ways of the forest have hunted and killed, and brought home for us."

Then the old warrior would cast away his pipe, smear the war paint on his unlovable, ferocious face, and take the warpath again.

But winter came, long, cold and dreary. The handsome young hunter sat in his lodge with luxury on every side. The thick hide of the moose formed the walls and roof of his dwelling. No wind could penetrate it, no heat from the sparkling fire escape from within. Exquisite furs, the pelts of the black bear, the red fox, the silver lynx, covered the floor and lay heaped in soft piles ready for his couch. On the hot stones about the fire baked and sizzled savory meats—bear steaks, strips from the haunch of deer—and in a stone vessel steamed soup made from the rich jelly of the tail of the beaver.

"I perish with cold," came a voice from outside. "I have tasted no food for two days. I am a stranger. Will you let me in?"

Instantly the hunter sprang to his feet, flung back the moose hide door, and stood, looking not at a stranger, but face to face with his enemy. The old warrior did not see into whose lodge he was stumbling, but crouched by the fire, warming his half-frozen body and sniffing at the roasting meats. Presently he looked up. Above him towered the young hunter, smiling down at him and saying:

"So? You honor my poor lodge at last.

Then I make you welcome."

The half frozen, starving old fighter struggled to his feet. "*You?*" He fairly hurled the word. "*You?* I did not know it was to your lodge I had come. Well! You have your chance now, you fighter of little foxes and feeder of old women. You will fight me now, I suppose—now when I am weak and frozen and foodless. You are too cowardly to fight me in my strength."

"Yes, I will fight you now," laughed the tall young hunter, bending his great length to lift with strong, quiet fingers the bowl of steaming soup to place it before his enemy.

The old warrior caught his breath. "You offer me this!" he exclaimed. "This *beaver-tail soup!* This food that for a thousand years the Mohawks reserve as the dish to place only before most welcome, most honored guests?"

"I offer you this," replied the young hunter, "for you are welcome, and any guest that comes to me honors me."

"Then you will not fight me, even now, when you could conquer and kill me!" exclaimed his enemy.

"You forget," replied the hunter, "that our tribe holds that, in addition to beaver-tail soup being a dish of honor, even one's greatest enemy is safe as a child in its cradle-board, while he is one's guest. Does not our Mohawk law demand that our bitterest enemy, even should he be the slayer of our own sire, may seek shelter under our roof, but while there, even if he have his weapons of war outside, he is safe. Honor forbids us taking advantage of him."

The old warrior arose, and standing in the red glare of the firelight, said simply, "You are greater than I, not only in stature, but in heart. Let there be peace between us. I have had a crooked heart. I would it were straight like yours."

"Perhaps both our hearts were crooked, replied the young hunter, "both uneven. If we link them together, the crookedness will disappear, one will balance the other, and we will crown them both with the owl, whose watching eyes will guard evil from touching them, just as it guards the Council Fire. Drink, O brother of mine. The beaver tail soup speaks the Mohawk word of welcome."

So the thought was born that grew, and was perpetuated in the Silver Brooch of Brotherhood.

THE BROOCH OF DREAMS

SOMETIMES THIS QUAINT LITTLE DESIGN is called "Heart of the Night," for the owl is a night bird, and this brooch is so perfect an owl that it would be impossible to mistake it for anything else; yet if the finger tip is laid over the beak and eyes, only a faultless heart remains, with no hint of a bird in its construction.

The Indians place a great value on this brooch, for it is supposed to have guardian powers. The beautifully simple faith of the redman has complete confidence in the idea that this particular emblem will prevent the approach of evil in the night hours. In the daylight it has no effect, but in the darkness it protects one from harm and hurt, and has the additional charm of giving to the sleeper pleasant and desirable dreams. It was, in fact, a dreamer who first designed "The Heart of the Night," and the romance of his experience, the marvel of his achievements, appealed so strongly to the marvel-loving Mohawks that they included this brooch among their important national emblems.

The "dreamer" was a young and very handsome boy, the son of a great medicine man, in whose footsteps the boy meant to follow. While he was yet very little, this boy learned about all the medicinal roots, herbs, barks and berries, the healing gums, the strengthening saps of trees, and he learned the chants and incantations, the dances and magical songs, that the Indian medicine men have used for centuries. Unlike most children, he never had any fear of the dark; from his earliest babyhood he ever showed contempt for it, for very great intelligence seemed to develop in him while yet a mere infant. As soon as he could toddle about, he would watch the sunset, and with the descending dusk of nightfall he would escape from his parents and brothers and creep away into the edge of the forest where the shadows were deepening, and until the home voices were heard calling him, he would remain buried in thought while the darkness shut him in like a wall, but no thought of fear ever occurred to him. When he learned to talk, he explained this odd baby truantism by the astonishing statement that he could see everything in the forest as well by night as by day, and that the owls, who never moved about in the daylight, always came near to "talk" to him in the shadows of night. Their great, all-seeing eyes were wonderfully luminous, and when they would hoot about and above him, they seemed to say, "Have no fear of us, oh! little Red Medicine Man. We are your brothers, and we love you. We will teach you to see in the dark just as we see, to find your food in the dark just as we find ours, to escape your enemies in the dark just as we escape ours. Come to us in the night hours, and we shall teach you these things."

When his parents heard this pretty tale, they let him alone, to wander as he would, and to learn all that his little brothers, the owls, could teach him. While he was yet a young boy, he made his own medicine masks and turtle shell "rattles," with which he was going to "cure" the sick when he grew up, and then, one day, he slipped away into the forest, built himself a rough log lodge, killed a few beasts, smoked and dried their flesh for food, used their skins for beds and blankets, and devoted himself to the study of his life—that of benefiting the sick and afflicted of his tribe. He had no companions but his friends, the owls, from which he learned the wisdom of being alert and watchful through the night hours.

Then, as time drifted on, the people of his tribe began to observe that sometimes in a single night miraculous cures took place, particularly among the children. Sometimes a little child would go to bed tossing with fever, shivering with ague, to awake in the morning bright-eyed and laughing, in perfect health. Children who feared the dark, and were troubled with nightmares, were suddenly cured of these disorders. Babies who had wailed through the endless night hours ceased their crying and slept peacefully and healthfully until sunrise.

"Who is doing all this? Who is giving the

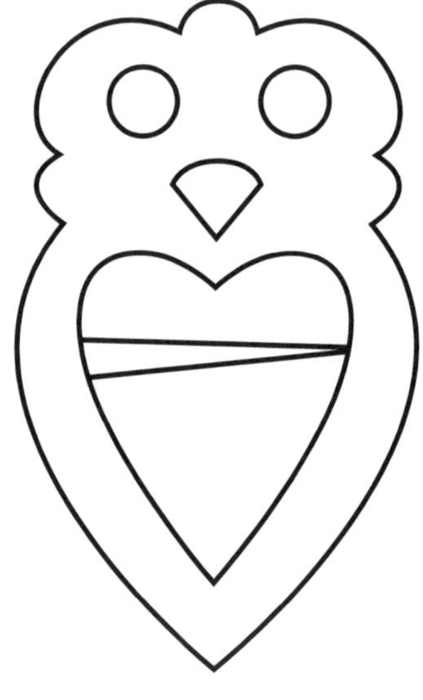

THE BROOCH OF DREAMS

blessing of silence and peace and health to our little ones? Who is it makes nightfall a welcome guest instead of a dreaded thing in our lodges and wigwams?" asked the old people of the Mohawks. But no one could make reply, for no one knew from what strange cause this sorcery sprang. Then followed still more wonderful enchantments. Sleepers began to be visited by the most blissful dreams; visions of herds of buffalo in vast hunting grounds came to the men of the Mohawks. Antelope and caribou in countless thousands raced and cantered through their dreams, until they awoke with regret from such alluring sights and joys of the chase. To the sleeping women came dreams of possessing numberless rabbit skin blankets, ermine garments, and immense stores of dried fish and smoked venison hams. The night hours became dreams of delight to all. And then one gray spring dawn the young medicine man left his forest retreat and rejoined his people.

"Oh, kinsmen of mine," he called, "have the nights proved beautiful to you? Have your children slept peacefully? Have your hearts and bodies rested happily? Have your dreams been of beauty? Has the darkness lost its gloom for you?"

And the people of his tribe crowded about him with welcoming, outstretched hands, for now they knew from what source all these blessings had come, and they proclaimed him as the Big Medicine Man of the Mohawks. In vain he told them that he had learned his witchcraft from his little brothers, the owls. They clamored that it was his own unselfishness in living alone to chant his incantations, to dance his medicine dances for the good of his people, that gave him his great powers of curing and healing. Then, amid great feasting and rejoicing, the silversmiths beat out this little brooch, and fastening it on his buckskin shirt, directly above his unselfish young heart, they cried:

"This will be his totem, for he lives to benefit his people. He will be the 'Heart of the Night,' and his heart, they cried: "He will be the 'Heart of the Night': The Brooch of Dreams."

THE HUNTER'S HEART

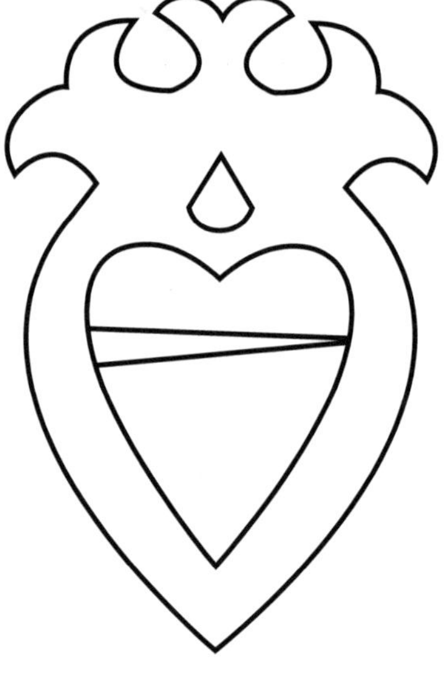

THE HUNTER'S HEART

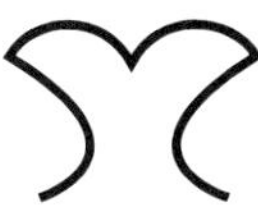

THERE IS NO BROOCH SO EARNESTLY DESIRED by the growing Mohawk boy as "The Hunter's Heart," for where can one find the boy, either white or red, who does not long to be a good shot, a successful angler or an expert trapper? That this little brooch will bring all these attainments is the serious belief of the Indian boy who is having his first experience in wresting food from the forest, and fish from the river. Here is our old time emblem, the silver heart, but in this case crested with the antlers of the deer, a most significant totem, for the antlers are used as a mark of chieftainship, and the little Mohawk hunter, whether born to chief's blood or without it, hopes that at least he may be "chief" among hunters, even if his ancestry does not proclaim him of the blood royal. Once more, by closing with a pencil mark the two gaps between the antlers, a perfect owl will be formed, with a cute little beak and full, heart shaped breast. Sometimes this brooch is called "The Heart of the Forest," for there is an idea connected with it that the wearer of it will have good fortune follow him only while he hunts in wooded or timbered places. It is one of the simplest designs the silversmith makes, but its manufacture is surrounded with much mystery. First, the workman insists upon absolute isolation while he melts and beats the precious silver, then forms it into this little ornament that will so gladden and strengthen the spirit of the hunter, for the wild things of the forest are more easily captured by the man who hunts alone, when there is no speech to alarm them, no noise but the almost inaudible one of approaching moccasined feet. So the maker of "The Hunter's Heart" wishes to weld loneliness into its folds of metal, wishes no other human presence about him to disturb the quiet that must reign while his slender fingers form and fashion this bit of silver beauty, that will bring joy to some eager boy stringing his bow for the first time.

The silversmith works very silently at his task. He melts and presses this brooch as much as possible, avoiding the loud beating and hammering which seems almost necessary to the making of other brooches. "Silence," is his work-word, for "silence" is the royal road to all success as a hunter. Whoever heard of a noisy fisherman or a chattering deer-stalker bringing home a bag of game?

"Seal your lips when you wear this," the old hunters say to the younger. "Step silently, breathe so that no man hears you, break no twigs, crush no leaves, splash no water, in your quest for wild food, or you will go hungry, and this brooch of The Hunter's Heart cannot help you."

So after all, it is not merely a suggestion that the brooch must be manufactured in silence, for the very presence of the emblem on his buckskin tunic would constantly remind the youthful hunter that "Silence" must be his motto, if he would win success.

It takes a long time and much experience for the Indian boy to master all the niceties of wood and water craft—to make and set traps so carefully that the wise creatures of the wilderness cannot scent the touch of a human hand about the snare; to know the tracks and haunts, the runways and stamping grounds of animals, the flights and cries of birds, the retreats and habits of fishes. He must learn when and when not to light a fire, when to pursue untiringly, and when to cease should the pursuit become dangerous. He must know the winds, the storms, the signs of coming waterfalls and rapids in the river; he must be familiar with the sun, the shadows, the stars, the ever changing moon, which holds such disaster or such promise for the hunter; he must be able to foretell threatening weather—a mild or severe winter, an early or belated spring; he must learn the poisonous plants and berries, so as to avoid them should his chase be unfortunate and he be driven to subsist on the slender fare gathered from bush and vine; he must know the warning signs of nearing vipers and stinging insects' nests, and must be familiar with the valuable herbs that act as antidotes for poisons. He must be on the alert for every sound, sight, touch or scent that makes for either approaching danger or ultimate success, and above all this wealth of knowledge he must place that little watchword "Silence," if he ever means to become a mighty hunter.

Some of the Mohawks still have a tale of the making of the first Hunter's Heart. It happened one year so long ago that tradition does not even name the century. There had been an almost endless winter. Of game there was none, the caribou had starved in the extreme depths of snow, the rabbits were mere skeletons for want of buds to browse on, the partridge berries lay beneath tons of snow, and the birds starved and froze and died. In the Indian lodges food became scarcer and scarcer, the old people weakened, the children grew hungry-eyed, the mothers hopeless, the fathers helpless. Then at last, one clear, blue morning, a warm wind blew up from the south, and on its invisible wings a great flock of wild geese honked their way into the Northland. Spring had come, with its promise of food, of fish and water fowl. There was joy in the Indian lodges as the gray geese fell before the hunter's arrow, and the gnawing hunger of many weeks was appeased at last. And then one day the ice faded from the river, the waters danced in the sunlight, the fish, crowding upstream to spawn, leaped in countless numbers. In those long bygone ages there were not white man's hooks and lines, but the "catch" all had to be made at night time, when the canoes thronged the river, each with its jacklight high in the bow, each with its stalwart, standing figure directly behind the light, spear in hand ready to plunge it into the luckless fish, that fascinated by the flame, arose to the surface of the stream; each with its silent paddler astern, upon the twist of whose wrist depended the balance of the frail craft.

The pungent scent from the flaming pine knots that composed the jacklight filled the air; the soft whir and flutter of the ascending sparks was the only sound to be heard.

But this early spring night the fleet of canoes floated and drifted for hours. Not a spear was plunged, not a single fish secured, for none came to the call of the jacklights; it was as if the stream were unpeopled with its old time sturgeon and bass and luscious trout.

In the bow of the foremost canoe stood a splendid young Mohawk with spear in hand, while his brother plied the paddle astern. The spearsman had almost lost heart with the long, long wait. No gleaming fins, no silvery scales, cut the river waters. The spearsman had a mother at home whom he loved, a mother who had half starved through the long, foodless winter, and he had, too, a baby sister and a young boy brother. His father? Ah! long ago his father had gone to the Happy Hunting Grounds of the Indian's "Great Hereafter." As the young spearsman stood, longing and hoping that a fish would yet follow his lure, the resinous jacklight flared up, and the smoke curled aloft in two thin, blue, spiral ribbons, that, floating upwards, joined with a little "dip" as if the weight of their combined forces could not rise. These smoke ribbons had formed a perfect heart. At this moment the hoot of an owl came from far up in the forest. "O-ho-wa! O-ho-wa!" it said.

The spearsman turned to his brother the paddler. "It is the guardian owl," he said, and the smoke has twisted itself into a heart. Perhaps it is the Hunter's Heart, the heart that begs for game because one's mother, and little sister, and boy brother, are hungry.

At that moment the forty fishermen on the river plunged their spears into the deep waters. Each spear secured a great fat sturgeon to flap and flounder in the canoe. The river had yielded its treasure of fish, and the young spearsman whose jacklight smoke had twisted itself into a heart, went home rich with food for his dear ones; and when they had eaten, he sat long by the fire, and beat out of virgin silver the design of "The Hunter's Heart."

THE TRAITOR'S HEARTS

THE MOHAWKS HAVE NEVER BEEN a race to brand or punish the wrong-doer; their policy has always been to honor and reward the right-doer, thus holding up achievement as something to be desired, rather than evil as something to be avoided. The Mohawk boy is taught to desire to do great things, and his people hope that by implanting ambition they are crowding out any tendency he may have to fail in the honorable things of life.

There were no prisons, no punishments, among the primitive Indians, but there were eagle plumes and brooches of distinction for those who lived bravely and uprightly. The one exception to this rule was the mark of "The Crooked Hearts," which doomed a man to disgrace for all time should he prove faithless to his friend, or to his tribe. There are two designs of this "Branding Heart"—the one simply ornamented with the graceful but condemning curve to base, the other of similar design but surmounted by a crown. The "brand" of this crested heart was always placed on a man who had proved a traitor to his tribe, but the uncrowned heart held a still blacker significance, for the man who wore it had proved faithless to his friend, had betrayed another man, had placed himself beyond the pale of honorable association with his fellows—in short, had made himself an outcast and an exile. Every boy reader of these articles will

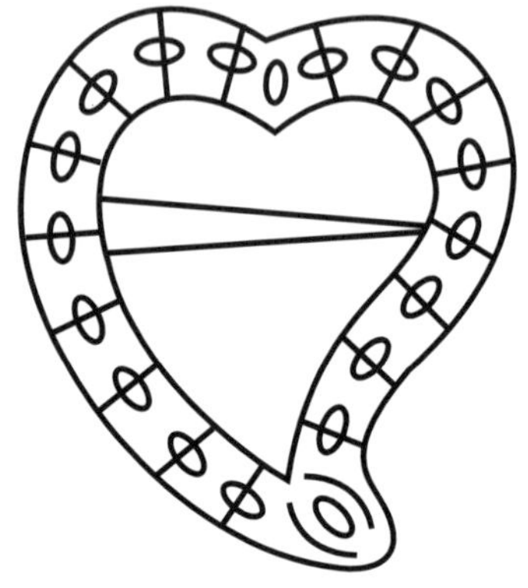

THE TRAITOR'S HEART

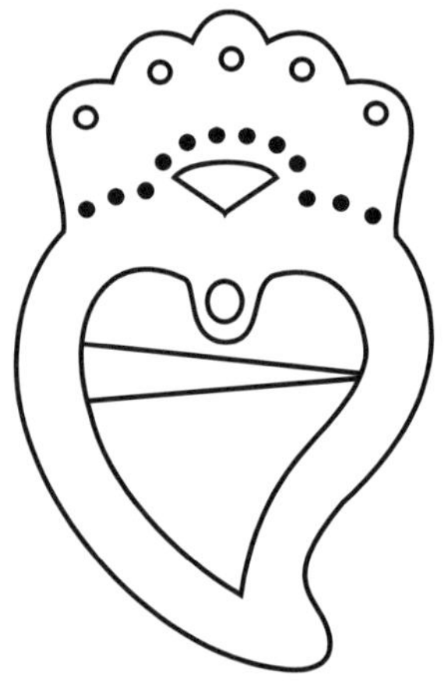

THE ROYAL TRAITOR'S HEART

readily understand how much rather the unfortunate man who was compelled to wear this heart, would have preferred to stand erect before the men of his tribe and be put to a heroic death by the arrows and tomahawks of his judges, but no such glory of martyrdom fell to his lot. His suffering was far worse than death, for he was allowed to live, to go about among his fellows, but not with them, wearing forever this little crooked heart to bar him from the respect of his tribesmen, and to brand him with the infamy of his treachery.

The "Royal" Traitor's Heart, as the crested one is called, was first fashioned for one whose very name was used for years as a synonym for perfidy. It was in the time of the mighty feuds between the Hurons and the Iroquois, sometime about the year 1620, when a score of Mohawk warriors were taken captive by the enemy and carried to a place of concealment. One by one these splendid fighters were taken before the War Council of the Hurons, and starved and tortured in the endeavor to make them reveal the plans of attack, and the hiding place of the Mohawk war party.

One by one these magnificent men laughed at, sneered at, and taunted their captors, then died with their lips still sealed in the noblest silence known to man. But at the very last, one recreant coward yielded; he divulged the plans, the tactics, the hiding place of his people, and was rewarded for his ignominy by being allowed to live. Following his lead the Hurons made a night attack upon the Mohawks. There was terrible slaughter on both sides, but the unfortunate renegade escaped death, and returned to his people, and, alas! to the unspeakable misery of being branded for life as a traitor to his race.

"Let us mark this snake of our tribe, so that all may know him as faithless," said the great Council of the Mohawks. "His heart is crooked, and he shall wear the symbol. Make a curved heart, surmount it with a crown, that all tribes and clans may never again entrust him with a state secret."

It is a little thing, this pretty silver heart, but it was worse than doom and death for the traitor who wore it.

Of the other, the uncrowned heart, there is yet another story, pitiful because of the human weakness that led to its first formation. There were two cousins of the "Bear" Clan, one with a very beautiful wife and two children; the other unmarried, and, according to the maidens of the tribe, likely to remain so. For, although he was very handsome and young and strong, he was also vain and indolent; he hated the warpath, hated the hunter's chase, hated anything that made him exert himself. He liked to loll about the great campfires, to smoke his pipe lazily, to eat great quantities of venison and rabbit stews, which the women prepared. He loved to paint his handsome face, and he always wore many chains of beautiful shell beads, of beaten silver, of bears' claws and elks' teeth. He amused the maidens, but they rather despised him, saying among themselves: "None of us will wed a man who wears all the necklaces and bracelets himself, who provides no food, and who would not fight for us in time of war."

The married cousin, on the contrary, was a splendid fellow. He got together a luxurious wigwam for his wife and children, costly furs, great heaps of tanned buckskins, a great supply of smoked fish and dried venison for the winter, rows and rows of strings of Indian corn. He was accounted wealthy, for he had a great herd of wild horses, and was known to have much silver buried somewhere in the forest, which he traded to other tribes for their valuables. It seemed odd that those two cousins so widely different in their dispositions should be firm and fast friends, but such ill-assorted companions can be found the world over.

When a war broke out, the unmarried cousin said he was ill—that he thought himself in the clutches of a death-dealing ague. So he still stayed lolling beside the campfires, while his cousin left wife and children and followed the warpath with the other warriors. But when the war party returned, with their ranks thinned, the warrior cousin was among the missing; he had died a valiant death at the hands of the enemy; his wife was alone, and his children fatherless. As soon as the news spread throughout the camp, and the voices of the women arose in the wailing death chant, the unmarried cousin hid himself away in his wigwam, and taking a roll of birch-bark he made hieroglyphics and tokens on it, signing it with the dead man's totem. Then he showed this scroll to the Council. It said that the dead warrior had left all his riches, his horses and silver and furs and foods to his cousin, and it was his request that, should he die in battle, his wife and children go home to live with her old father, from whence he had taken her as a bride. "This my cousin gave to me before he took the warpath," said the coward. "He knew I was ill, even at death's door. He wished me to die not in need." So the wife and children returned to her father, plunged into the depths of poverty. But after a time released captives began returning from the war. They had seen the warrior cousin die, had heard him tell over and over that all his wealth was for his wife and children. The Council began to grow uneasy, then demanded once more to see the birch-bark scroll. On examining closer they discovered it to be a fraud. The totem was plainly not the work of the dead warrior's hand. "He has proved false to his friend," they declared. "Bring back the wife and children to their own possessions, and mark this man forever as a traitor to another man's trust." Then the silversmiths beat out this crooked heart. The chiefs fastened it on the front of his buckskin shirt. "Traitor!" cried the maidens, pointing at him. "Traitor!" scowled the chiefs. "Traitor!" jeered the warriors. The miserable usurper could not escape from his dishonorable deed; it gleamed up at him, mocked him, day after day, in the radiance of the silver heart. Weeks, months, years, he lived to bear his doom, to wear this brand of faithlessness; for, like all men, whether Indian or white, the scar of a dishonorable deed was made to cling to him—he could never rid himself of this brand of the Crooked Heart.

THE SUN OF FRIENDSHIP

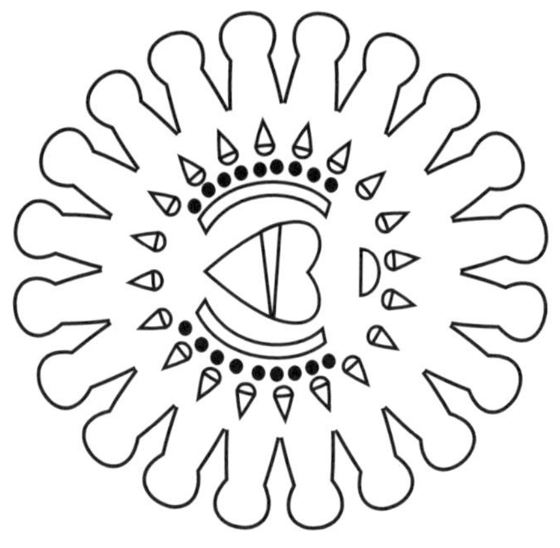

THE SUN OF FRIENDSHIP

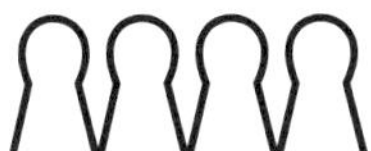

STRONGER THAN HIS HATE, stronger than his revenge, stronger than his love, stronger than death itself, is the friendship of a Red Indian.

Since time began, the Mohawks have always likened friendship to the sun. It is exalted in the high heavens, it is the power of heat, of light, of strength. Without the sun, this world would not continue to exist; without friendship, the Mohawk holds that the heart of mankind would be the bleached, colorless, bloodless thing that a plant is when grown in the dark.

"My friend and myself are one," the Mohawk says. "There cannot be two of us; we are of one heart encircled by the warm, light-giving rays of the sun." So, long ago, a noble, young, Indian silversmith beat out this brooch to illustrate the beliefs and sentiments of his race.

The reader will observe that this is the very largest silver brooch of the series, which shows the vast importance with which it is regarded by its makers and wearers. A breach of friendship is the most unpardonable crime known to a Mohawk's code of honor. We have already illustrated in what contempt it is held by the brand of the "Crooked Hearts."

There are many seemingly simple things that betoken friendship between men and tribes and families, but the most commonly observed is that if a man offers you food when you are hungry, and when you partake of that food in his wigwam, you are bound in friendship to him for all time. You must share your fortunes with him should he stand in need of it; you must fight for him, die for him if necessary; and the day when you forget that he has fed you when you were foodless, is the day of doom for you. You will be branded with the little crooked silver heart, and this beautiful, clear "circle of sun rays" brooch will be removed from your vesture for evermore.

But the man who wears this brooch can hold his head erect, he can look his forest world in the face, for honor is his, and uprightness and loyalty; he is indeed a man among men.

This brooch came to be fashioned in a curious manner. It will be noticed that, unlike all other brooches which form the heart design of the silver, this particular heart is—space, the metal being pierced out in that shape, not beaten in. The heart is a hollow space, empty and void, which means that the material human heart has gone; it is the heart of one dead, and the story is one of a man who was loyal to his dead friend, even when this loyalty was detrimental to his own interests.

There had been a long and terrible war between the Mohawks and the Cherokees. Two mighty nations matched one against the other, equal in prowess, in intrigue, in bravery.

Captives were taken by both tribes, battles won by both; victories, losses, hunger, famine, misery, haunted the forest like specters. Then came one terrible, decisive conflict; the mighty Mohawks won it—secured, as they thought, all their tribesmen taken captive by the Cherokees, and returned to their own country loaded with plunder and the spoils of war. But, hidden away in the depths of their wilderness territory, the wily Cherokees still held two Mohawk lads, one a young aristocrat just come into his title of "chief"; the other, not of noble blood, but who bore the significant name of "Ik-chen," which means "The Best," "The Strongest," "The Most Masterful," "The Leader."

These lads had been friends from their infancy. They had grown up together, hunted and fished together, and now it looked as if they were to die together.

The Cherokees were boastful with pride at outwitting the Mohawks. They held this most important young chief of the powerful "Wolf Clan" of their enemies. Of his friend, "Ik-chen," they thought little, as he was just a boy who could never sit in the Great Council of the Mohawks. He was not even of an important family. But of the young chief they planned to make great profit. They would follow the Mohawks, and, from some point of vantage, they would parley for "terms."

If the Mohawks would not return them

their plundered stores and treasures and their tribesmen still held captive in the Mohawk camps, they would heap indignities on the young chief, torture him and kill him before their very eyes.

"Ik-chen," with the ears of a lynx, overheard this plan, but stoically kept it to himself. "They shall not taunt my people, they shall not kill my friend," he vowed. "They have outwitted us proud Mohawks, but I shall outwit them; my people shall jeer and laugh at them yet!"

Then he formed within his brain a plan that few would dare to think twice of doing. The lads were of the same height, of much the same build and features. The main difference, to a careless observer, between the two, was only that the young chief wore ermine fringes to his sleeves and leggings, and used much brilliant paint on his face, as befitted his rank, while "Ik-chen" wore his brown furs and the unpainted face of one not of noble blood. That night, as they slept side by side, "Ik-chen" arose. Noiselessly he dressed himself, not in his own simple garments, but in the gorgeous ones of his friend, painted his face with the disguising black lines across the forehead, the brilliant scarlet on his cheeks, the black "necklace" rings about his throat. Then, rousing his friend, he said:

"While it is yet midnight you must escape. I have discovered the way. Stop not a moment;

dress rapidly, then run—run as the caribou, fly as the eagle, down the gorge, turn to your right three times; you will find the trail of our people; follow it. Ask me no questions. I shall join you to-morrow. Only hasten, hasten now, and remember, you owe it to the pride of the Mohawks that you outwit these enemies of ours. Hasten, again, hasten!"

The young chief sprang up. In the darkness he did not see that he was slipping on his friend's, not his own, garments.

"They think nothing of me," urged "Ik-chen," as his friend waited to protest at leaving him.

"They will let me go, but you they value. Hasten, oh, friend of my heart, hasten!"

"But I shall not stir unless you come with me," began the other.

"Hasten!" cried "Ik-chen." "I will roll myself in the bearskins so that they will think there are two of us yet, and you will have many hours' headstart on their following feet. Hasten!" And, with a firm hand, "Ik-chen" thrust his friend out into the night. But the captive boy did not "roll himself in the bearskins." He lay uncovered, so that his painted face and ermine-fringed garments could be plainly seen from the wigwam door, where, from time to time, his captors thrust watchful faces to see that their victims were safe.

"My friend has left me!" wailed "Ik-chen" in the morning, when the Cherokees threatened trouble because of only one captive in camp.

"It matters not!" they sneered. "Let him go; it is you, the chief of the arrogant Mohawks, that we desire to keep."

So the loyal heart of "Ik-chen" was at rest about his friend; and when, four days later, the Cherokees broke camp to follow the trail of the Mohawks, the lad walked bravely and silently in the captive's "bands," though knowing that, sooner or later, this tribe of vengeful warriors would discover how they had been deceived.

Across the river from the camp of victorious Mohawks they halted.

"Give us back those you have taken captive!" they demanded. "Give us back the treasures you have plundered, and you may have this stripling chief of yours—unharmed!" Then they raised "Ik-chen" to their shoulders, so that the Mohawks might see him—"Ik-chen," clad in the ermine, the scarlet and black paint of a chieftain.

"You have no chief of ours!" jeered back and laughed the Mohawks. "Our young chief has returned to us!"

"Oh, 'Ik-chen,' 'Ik-chen,' my friend, my fellow-captive, what is this that you have done to save me!" called the real chief, flinging himself towards the river shore, as he saw the boy, clad in his own disguising garments, surrounded by those giant enemies.

Instantly the enraged Cherokees saw how

they had been tricked; that the real chief had escaped them, and that they held only this untitled boy who, to them, was valueless. Like a flash, twenty arrows fled, buried to the feathers, in the boy's heroic, loyal young breast. "Ik-chen" had given his life for his friend.

Bowed with grief, the young chief refused even to be addressed by his title, or to sit in council. "I give my title to my dead friend, 'Ik-chen,'" he said. "He is more worthy of it than I. My heart is empty for evermore, for he has gone from me. Make me a silver symbol of friendship, of the sun's rays shining on a heart, but the heart must be like my own—empty!"

And this is the origin of "The Sun of Friendship."

ALSO FROM SUBWAY BOOKS

The Totem Poles Of Stanley Park

VICKIE JENSEN

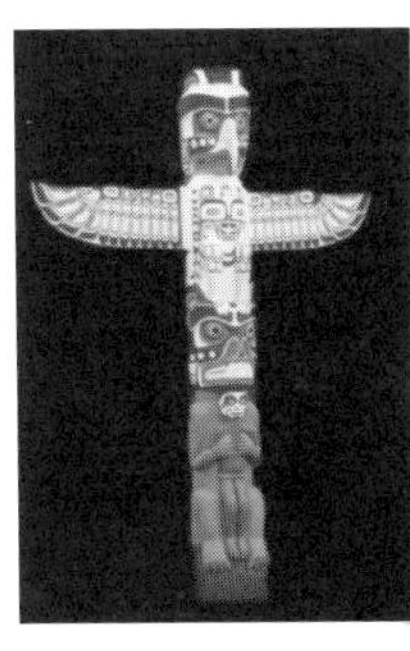

This is the first convenient guide to the totem poles in Vancouver's famous Stanley Park, which have fascinated visitors and locals since the 1920s and are now the most popular tourist attraction in British Columbia, drawing three million people a year. Combining lively text with abundant photographs, illustrations and maps, this pocket-sized guide describes and tells the story of each totem pole, explaining the figures represented and discussing the artists who created them. There's also basic information about totem poles in general—how and why they're carved and how the craft has changed over the generations. Readers can quickly learn to pick out common totemic or crest figures and familiarize themselves with other basic features of these monumental carvings.

ISBN: 0-9687163-8-5 • $9.95 PAPER

SUBWAY BOOKS • WESTCOAST WORDS